NOTES ON FUGUE

for

BEGINNERS

BY
THE LATE
E. J. DENT

CAMBRIDGE
AT THE UNIVERSITY PRESS
1958

CAMBRIDGE
UNIVERSITY PRESS

University Printing House, Cambridge CB2 8BS, United Kingdom

Published in the United States of America by Cambridge University Press, New York

Cambridge University Press is part of the University of Cambridge.

It furthers the University's mission by disseminating knowledge in the pursuit of
education, learning and research at the highest international levels of excellence.

www.cambridge.org
Information on this title: www.cambridge.org/9781107629547

© Cambridge University Press 1958

Privately printed 1941
First published by the Syndics of the Cambridge University Press 1958
First published 1958
First paperback edition 2014

A catalogue record for this publication is available from the British Library

ISBN 978-1-107-62954-7 Paperback

PREFACE

These pages are intended for beginners who are making their very first attempts at fugue. I have not set out to write a complete treatise on fugue, nor even a concise compendium of its rules. I have assumed that the reader will be working regularly under a teacher, or at least teaching himself from one of the standard text-books, and all I offer him are a few marginal notes and comments.

The best text-book of fugue is the *Traité de Fugue* of André Gédalge (Paris, Enoch & Co.). It deals solely with the *fugue d'école* or 'examination fugue', but in fullest detail. The best English book is that of Ebenezer Prout (London, Augener & Co.); not very imaginative, but extremely broad-minded, with examples from a wide range of composers. In connexion with Prout's *Fugue*, the same author's *Double Counterpoint* and *Fugal Analysis* (Augener) should be carefully studied.

Owing to the expense of music-printing, I have had to do without musical examples in these pages, except for a few that I have had printed in Tonic Sol-Fa. If the reader cannot sing at sight from Tonic Sol-Fa, it is high time that he set to work to learn it, whatever his age and dignity may be.

E. J. D

WHY SHOULD WE STUDY FUGUE?

There are many very musical people to whom the word fugue suggests nothing more than a dreary exhibition of tiresome pedantry. The same people will probably listen to *Messiah* with the greatest pleasure, blissfully unaware that many of its choruses are fugues. They hear the words and are guided by them to an appreciation of Handel's constructive and expressive genius. The fugues that have frightened them away are more probably those of J. S. Bach which they have heard played on the organ as they walk out of church, already in a state of boredom and anxious to get home to Sunday dinner.

Teachers talk of fugue as a discipline, and that odious word is enough to make any musician, young or old, resentful of it. In old days, fugue of an elaborately academic type was considered indispensable to the equipment of a church musician, so that when Rossini said to his teacher that he did not want to be a church musician and knew enough to compose operas he was merely showing common sense. All the same, Rossini was an accomplished contrapuntist.

The chief reason for studying fugue nowadays is that it is the one type of music that has never gone out of fashion since it first came in. Even in the age of the great symphonies, Haydn, Mozart and Beethoven were masterly fugue-writers. In the 19th century it was not so much the rather academic-minded Brahms who wrote fugues as the ultra-romantic Berlioz, Schumann and Liszt. Coming down to more modern times we find remarkable fugues written by Verdi, César Franck, Richard Strauss, Ravel, Busoni, Hindemith, not to mention our own English composers. The classical forms of cantata, aria, sonata, &c., as well as the romantic rhapsodies and symphonic poems, have their day and disappear; fugue remains, and continues to fascinate composers. They do

7

not write as many fugues now as in the days of **Handel** and **J. S. Bach**, but they reserve their fugues for occasions of peculiarly concentrated emotional expression. Fugue has for many generations had the reputation of being 'academic', but at all periods there have been great musicians who were able to make it the vehicle of intense feeling and passion.

At the same time the construction of a fugue is a highly intellectual process; for this reason it is a valuable training to a young musician in applying conscious brain-work to composition, and if he studies fugue in the right way he will soon discover that no amount of conscious brain-work is much use without an intense concentration of the emotional imagination as well.

HISTORY OF FUGUE

Fugue comes from the Latin word *fuga*, which originally meant flight, or running away; in the Middle Ages *fuga* meant not what we now call a fugue, but a strict canon, and canon (Greek, *kanon*) meant a *rule*. If two or more people are to sing a canon, it need only be written out once, provided a direction is given at what points the successive voices are to enter. Mediaeval composers often made this direction mysterious and enigmatical, and this is what the word *canon* originally meant.

Canon as a musical device is much older than fugue. The oldest known canon is the famous *Sumer is icumen in* (*c.* 1260), which is called in the original manuscript neither *canon* nor *fuga*, but *rota* (wheel), which is what we now call a *round*. In England we have for several centuries distinguished between *rounds, catches* and *canons*: other languages seem to call them all canons indiscriminately. A round is a canon in which the voices enter only at the ends of definite rhythmical periods, as in *Sumer is icumen in* and *Three blind mice*. In the 18th century rounds were sometimes written on the Continent with much longer intervals between the voices, a whole stanza instead of a single line, e.g. the canon sung in the supper-scene of Mozart's opera *Così fan Tutte* (Act II) or that in the first act of Beethoven's *Fidelio*.

A great deal of 13th-century church music sounds roughly like an interminable extension of *Sumer is icumen in*, with two or three voices singing jiggy tunes on a stagnant bass, and constantly exchanging parts, as in a round. A little melodic phrase of about three or five notes will be passed from one voice to another, and a continuous series of these exchanges will be developed. Here we see what is partly a sort of canon, and partly a sort of *ground*, leading eventually to such works as Taverner's Mass *The Western Wynde*, where a very secular tune is repeated over and over again by various voices in turn, and Byrd's ground *The leaves be green*, where the ground theme (again a secular tune) is not confined to the bass as in a *ground bass* but is passed to each instrument in turn. This often happens too in Purcell's compositions on a ground. The connexion is interesting because it seems to be a peculiarly English device.

The music of the *ars antiqua* (13th century), which was almost always in three-beat measures, was mainly constructed on principles which must originally have been entirely haphazard—strict canon and *quodlibet*. The *quodlibet* type is the mediaeval *motet*, in which three voices sing quite different tunes to different words, sometimes even in different languages—the aim being to secure concords of octaves or fifths on the main beats and let the rest clash as it might.

In the 14th century we have the *ars nova*, still mainly in three parts, but preferring two-beat measures, and gradually learning to appreciate the consonances of the third and sixth. This was a great age of strict canon, exemplified best in the *caccia* (Italian, *chase*, or *hunt*), a long composition for two voices in canon with an independent bass. The words of these are generally cheerful,

9

often humorous, dealing with sport, country life, &c. They are descriptive scenes rather than songs, and were mostly composed at Florence. The *caccia* went out of fashion before the end of the 14th century. Note that this was the period of Dante, Petrarch and Boccaccio.

In the 15th century there is more tendency to four-part harmony, and there came a moment when the full rich sound of chords in four parts, singing music that to us sounds like the simplest hymn tunes, was a startling novelty. At the same time musicians discovered the advantages of free imitation. They still practised strict canon, and in the most elaborate and complicated forms, but it is evident that these devices, cultivated by the learned Netherlanders, did not much appeal to the general musical public. There was a great reaction in favour of block harmony.

The most popular form in the 15th century was the *chanson* (French, *song*), a simple song harmonized generally for four voices with elementary contrapuntal imitations. We now reach the period when the principal melody is transferred gradually from the tenor to the treble. The methods of secular music were applied (as in all centuries) to church music, and the form of the *chanson* was followed in the settings of Latin hymns by Cavazzoni, Victoria, Palestrina and others. Each strain of the hymn tune was introduced by a series of free imitations in the subsidiary voices.

The *chanson* was the ancestor of three musical families. It might be regarded as (1) a rhythmical melody, (2) a setting of words, or (3) a piece of counterpoint. If we regard melody as the main thing, a tune sung to be danced to, the *chanson* leads on to all instrumental dance forms and thus to pure instrumental music such as *suites*, *symphonies* and *sonatas*.

If the words are the main thing, it leads on to the *madrigal* and the *opera*.

10

If the counterpoint is the main thing, it leads first to the *canzona* (Italian form of the word *chanson*), which is an instrumental form consisting of a series of fugal expositions strung together and united by the fact that the subjects, taken by themselves, form a continuous tune. Gradually the continuous tune breaks up, and unity is attained by confining the development to one main subject. At this point the form we now call a *fugue* emerges, and the composer who contributed most to its creation is probably Girolamo Frescobaldi (1583–1643).

Instrumental fugue, sometimes for the organ, sometimes for strings or other instruments, was the main form of the 17th century. It had developed out of vocal fugue, but just at this moment there came a great expansion of instrumental music in all European countries. The 17th century was a great era of engineering and therefore of organ-building, and the construction of large organs, especially in Protestant Germany, led naturally to the organ fugues of Buxtehude and J. S. Bach.

At the same time it should be noted that in the 17th century all music which is not definitely dance music, song, or some kind of improvisation (prelude, toccata, &c.), is fugal in style. The favourite forms are the fugal overture (Lully, Purcell, &c.), the fugal sonata for two violins (Corelli and his predecessors), the fugal duet for two singers (Scarlatti, &c.); and it is noticeable that even in solo music, even in opera, composers are so much in the habit of thinking fugally that they construct their melodies by making one same voice sing both a subject and its answer. Handel and J. S. Bach are both rather isolated figures. Handel in London went on composing in the Scarlattian style, and Bach at Leipzig in that of Frescobaldi, long after the younger generation (including Bach's own sons) had adopted the more modern style associated with the classical sonata and symphony. The style dominated by fugal principles came to an end about 1750, and after that fugue is regarded rather as a dead language like Latin, appropriate mainly to the church. There are now two distinct types of fugue, existing indeed since about 1650 or earlier—the Catholic vocal fugue designed for the requirements of the liturgy, and the Protestant organ fugue free of all restrictions. Mozart must compress his vocal fugues as concisely as he can, because the archbishop is gouty and does not like standing; Bach's congregation will let him ramble away to eternity, because they may listen to him sitting down or can go out when they are bored.

Mozart tells us in his letters that he loved extemporizing fugues at the organ, and the fugue has always been a favourite form of the great improvisers. You who read these lines are probably an organist and extemporize in public every Sunday, perhaps weekdays too. How often do you extemporize fugues?

Mozart produced some very remarkable fugues of a sombre and almost terrifying type in his later years. Beethoven's fugues are numerous and the three huge fugues in B flat represent him at the summit of his genius. Schubert and Spohr seem to have written fugues as a matter of duty, Mendelssohn as a matter of respectability. Schumann's fugues are a humble homage to the newly rediscovered Bach. Berlioz made fun of academic fugues, but wrote astonishingly expressive ones far more often than most of his critics imagine.

Other interesting fugues of the later 19th century are Liszt's organ fugue on the chorale from Meyerbeer's opera *Le Prophète*, and the orchestral fugue in his symphonic poem *Prometheus*. Boito, probably remembering the fugue at the end of Berlioz's *Fantastic Symphony*, wrote a very exciting fugue for the witches and devils in his opera *Mefistofele*. There are original and expressive fugues by Verdi in his String Quartet and in his *Requiem*; his comic opera *Falstaff* ends with a deliberately formal fugue, suggested perhaps by the fugal entries of the finale of Mozart's *Don Giovanni*.

THE ACADEMIC STUDY
OF FUGUE

Ebenezer Prout, when he first published his text-book of fugue in 1891, thought himself a very daring revolutionary for suggesting that J. S. Bach ought to be regarded as the supreme authority on fugue. Even as late as 1920 Charles Koechlin in Paris felt himself to be equally audacious for suggesting the same thing to orthodox French teachers. English students of the present day, who seem to be better acquainted with J. S. Bach than with any other classical composer, may well be surprised at such an attitude. But the Bach movement in England is mainly a growth of the last fifty years, and was created by the enthusiasm of Walter Parratt, H. P. Allen and W. G. Whittaker. France and Italy are still very far behind in knowledge of Bach, and even in Germany the Bach movement was for more than one hundred years after Bach's death limited to scholars and academic circles. When Prout wrote his book, the chief authority on counterpoint and fugue for England was Ouseley, whose treatise is based mainly on Cherubini and the French and Italian authorities. Macfarren is said to have regarded Bach's fugues as most dangerous examples to students.

Macfarren was not far wrong, if he was thinking of absolute beginners, for the '48', to say nothing of the great organ fugues, have little in common with the orthodox *fugue d'école*, as Gédalge calls it—what we may call the academic examination fugue. But the academic fugue has a very honourable ancestry in the church fugues of Mozart and his Italian models, and it is far the best model for the beginner.

A student who is anxiously preparing for an examination is easily tempted to think that fugue is an affair of antiquated rules and purely mechanical construction, a thing useless for any purpose except the obtaining of an academic degree; and that when once he has obtained this degree he will never want to write another fugue in his life.

It is urgently important to realize from the outset that fugue is a most powerful means of emotional expression. As we proceed to the study of its component details we shall see that every single one of them is ultimately determined by considerations of feeling and emotion. It is fatal to begin the study of fugue by writing mere paper fugues according to rule without any thought of what they would sound like when sung or played and without any indications of tempo or expression. It is true that certain details have to be practised separately, and indeed mechanically, just as a pianist has to practise certain finger exercises; but these studies are subsidiary to composition, and a new interest may often be given to them by making them conscious studies in expression as well as in ingenuity.

Handel, J. S. Bach and their contemporaries wrote fugues in such quantity that fugue, with them, may easily seem to be little more than a matter of routine, and it is difficult for a beginner to make a selection from their works which he can study intensively as examples of emotional expression. It is easier to pick examples from composers who wrote in fugue more rarely.

Here are a few chosen to illustrate specific emotional characteristics. They are not necessarily complete fugues; some are merely short fugatos, but none the less expressive.

Rage and despair: Haydn, *The Creation*, No. 3—'Despairing, cursing rage &c.' Mozart, Fugue in C minor for two pianofortes.

Horror: Schumann, *Requiem*, 'Dies irae'.

Agony: Verdi, *Requiem*, 'Libera me, Domine'.

Steadfast endurance: Mozart, *The Magic Flute*, Act ii, Duet for Two Men in Armour. César Franck, fugue in *Prélude, Choral et Fugue*.

14

Ecstatic contemplation: Berlioz, *Childhood of Christ*, Epilogue.

Erotic desire: D. Scarlatti, 'The Cat's Fugue'. Tradition says that the subject of 'The Cat's Fugue' was suggested by a cat walking on the keys of a harpsichord. Practical experiment will show that this is impossible. It is much more reasonable to interpret the subject as representing the cat's nocturnal cry.

Mirth and mockery: Beethoven, String Quartet in C minor, Op. 18, Scherzo. Verdi, *Falstaff*, Epilogue.

GENERAL PRACTICE

In composing a fugue it is a good plan to provide oneself with two separate sheets of music-paper. Other useful accessories are (1) a good pencil, (2) a pencil sharpener, (3) a good piece of indiarubber. Pen and ink are only for those who can write a faultless fugue straight away with no need to correct it.

Use one sheet for the composition of the fugue itself and the other for rough work and the solution of small problems. Begin on the rough sheet (several may ultimately be wanted) by trying out subjects and their right answers, counter-subjects of various kinds. Try out at once all the possibilities that can be discovered in subject, answer and counter-subject of imitation, canon, *stretto*, also of inversion, *cancrizans* if you think it worth while, augmentation and diminution.

Collect material for episodes, using fragments derived from the subject, answer and counter-subject and experimenting with sequences and triple counterpoint.

All this takes some time and much indiarubber as well as patience and ingenuity; but it is absolutely necessary. Needless to say all this work will be done on the rough sheets.

15

We may begin to compose our exposition on the clean sheet, but the moment we find ourselves in difficulties we must turn to the other and work our problem out on that. It is sometimes useful *not* to rub out all mistakes on the rough sheet, but to make a fresh start; in this way we can observe the steps by which we have improved our work. Besides, if a combination will not work in the place where we want it, it may possibly work somewhere else, and it is a pity to rub it out and forget it.

Gédalge advises the examination candidate to begin by making these preliminary studies, then to write the exposition, and after that the final section, leaving the middle section to be composed last. This method may have some advantages when time is limited. If the candidate cannot write the whole fugue in the time allowed, most examiners would probably prefer to see a beginning and an end without a middle than a beginning and middle without an end. One might say that the exposition is a test of skill, the middle section a test of imagination and the final section a test of both. If knowledge of 'rules' and mere ingenuity is all that examiners want, they may be content with fragments. If expressive character and real musical invention are to be shown, it is probably more practicable to compose the fugue straight ahead, unless the candidate is so accomplished that he can conceive the whole fugue in his head complete.

It is certainly a good plan, when starting on a fugue, especially in an examination, to form some sort of general idea in one's head as to what the treatment should be; and that will include an idea of what the end should be, whether loud or soft, triumphal or despairing, ingeniously complex or deliberately simple as a relief from complications in the middle section. In such cases it is not altogether impracticable to follow Gédalge's advice. The end is made safe in good time, and the amount of time still available may determine how many entries and episodes can be used in the middle section. If the number of entries has to be reduced to two, their keys must be carefully chosen in order to secure proper balance. The choice, in such a case, will depend largely on the expressive character, e.g. whether major or minor keys should be chosen, or one of each.

The final bars of a fugue are often difficult to write. It is not always practicable, nor even always desirable, to keep the thematic material going up to the very end; but if this is not done, the beginner should do his best to avoid commonplace and conventional extensions of the *coda* derived from second-rate religious music and suggesting the reverent rubbish that an organist extemporizes to give the clergy time to settle comfortably into their seats.

Every student will have to find out for himself the method of work which suits his own temperament the best, and I have no wish to lay down any one method as the best. But if I may offer him an old examiner's advice, I would at any rate beg him to make every effort to show up a fugue that is finished and complete, whatever its length may be.

FUGUES FOR VOICES

It is advisable to begin writing fugues for voices, *with words*, as soon as possible. The French *fugue d'école* is really a vocal fugue in substance, though it has no words.

The importance of setting words is: (1) It concentrates attention on the fundamental principle that fugue must be *expressive*. (2) It helps to shape phrases, both in subjects and in countersubjects. This is often difficult, but can be overcome. (3) The phrases being shaped by the form of the words, they come to an end; and thus the bass is able to leave off for rests, and the other voices too. If there are no words, it is often extremely difficult to make the voices leave off, especially the bass, which soon degenerates into a 'table-leg bass', i.e. one which supports the harmony but has no interest of its own. The association of words also helps us to observe the old rule that a voice should never enter except on a point of imitation, or with some definite subject that is part of the fugal structure. The old composers of the 17th and 18th centuries were extremely strict about this; indeed, their music would lead us to believe that they simply could not conceive of a part entering with mere fill-up material.

It may seem natural to us nowadays to write vocal fugues (for performance) in at least four parts; and four-part fugue is too difficult for beginners. But the old composers wrote vocal fugues in two parts (on a short plan)—sometimes as *solfeggi* or studies for singers. It is quite possible to make them expressive and beautiful. A plan for a short fugue of this type is given later.

Three-part fugues for voices should best be written in fairly close harmony for voices of the same type, e.g. for women's voices, as in a convent choir (S.S.A.), or for men's voices, including the English combination A. (male) T.B. Care must be taken to consider *tessitura*, quality of voices in different registers, and compass, also distance of voices apart. Remember that a female contralto does not make as firm a bass as a male bass does, and that music for female voices must be chary of progressions needing strong dominant harmony (root in bass): it should tend more to first inversions than to root positions.

Vocal fugues will generally depend on subjects rather than on episodes; they may even have no episodes at all, interest being maintained by *stretto* and combinations of subjects.

Instrumental fugues lean more to episode (cf. J. S. Bach's organ fugues). In writing instrumental fugues, consider carefully for what instrument or combination of instruments they are conceived. The temptation of most students will be to write for organ. They should be reminded that in the whole of J. S. Bach's organ works there is not one example of a complete three-part fugue for two manuals and pedal, though in the greater fugues there are often episodes for this combination. If three-part fugues are written for the organ with pedals, the parts must move with a great deal of freedom, and be strongly individualized. This is very difficult for beginners. It is better to try a type in closer and quieter harmony, more like a vocal fugue, perhaps *manualiter*, in which case care must be taken to avoid wide stretches and things uncomfortable to play.

At a certain stage it is a very good plan to write two-part fugues for violins, or for violin and viola, especially on rapid subjects with a great many semiquavers. Three-part fugues for violin, viola and violoncello are not satisfactory in sound unless (like three-part organ fugues) they have very strongly individualized parts with great freedom of movement.

FUGUES FOR PIANOFORTE

The '48' are not good models for beginners. They are almost all very difficult to play, and are conceived more for harpsichord or organ than for a modern pianoforte. The moment real pianoforte technique comes into consideration, the problem of fugue becomes immensely difficult and complicated. Stanford said that all pianoforte writing was fundamentally two-part: and this is more or less the case in Brahms's fugue at the end of the Handel variations. This is also characteristic of D. Scarlatti's keyboard fugues. A really good pianoforte fugue is almost inevitably compelled to be a fake fugue, i.e. one that could not be put into score; and before a composer can write fake fugues properly he must certainly obtain mastery of the genuine fugue.

It is most important that students should never allow themselves to write 'paper' fugues, conceived merely as exercises in abstract sound regardless of practical conditions of performance.

19

SUBJECT

There are two standard types of subject: (1) expressive, (2) formal. In type (1) the composer is concentrated on personal and poetical expression; the emotional character of the fugue is inherent in the subject and the whole fugue must be planned round this expression. Subjects of type(2) are often fragments of plainsong in white notes. Here the main interest is architectural, in the construction and building up of the fugue with all sorts of counter-subjects, canons and imitations, &c. (e.g. C sharp minor fugue of '48', Book I).

This is naturally the more difficult kind of fugue to write, and the beginner will do well to start on the expressive type.

A fugue ought always to have some definite character as a piece of music, to be, e.g. cheerful or melancholy, solemn or frivolous (the architectural fugues belong mostly to the solemn and dignified kind); it should announce this character in the subject itself, maintain it more or less throughout and carry it on to the end. Hence it is most important to invent really expressive subjects; this is really far more vital than the question of whether they will work in *stretto* or inversion, &c. Avoid fugue subjects which merely sound like fugue subjects and nothing else; and practise inventing your own rather than take subjects out of old examination papers. Examiners generally set subjects which have some sort of an awkward catch in them, to see whether a candidate can find the correct answer; and very often they will not even work happily in *stretto*.

Old Italian writers on fugue distinguished between a *soggetto* and an *andamento* (see Grove's *Dictionary* for definition). Roughly speaking the *soggetto* is what Gédalge calls the 'head of a subject' and the *andamento* (literally, a walking or going) is what we may call the 'tail'. A great many classical subjects will divide obviously in this way into head and tail, but not all. The division is important in view of the answer.

THE ANSWER

Fugue having begun as a series of imitations sung by voices of different pitch, it was natural that the second voice should enter with the subject a fifth or fourth above or below the first. In the course of generations it became the regular rule that the answer to the subject should be made in the key of the dominant, i.e. either a fifth above or a fourth below. With the gradual development of classical tonality in the 16th and 17th centuries it became customary (but not a fixed rule) to modify the subject in the answer, so that if the subject itself (as often happens) led towards the dominant, the answer should lead back from the dominant to the tonic. If the answer were exact, it would then lead towards its own dominant, i.e. the supertonic of the original key, which would make it awkward for the third voice (presumably an octave above or below the first) to enter in the original key.

This alteration of the subject (sometimes called *mutation*) is a source of much difficulty to beginners. If the subject is not altered at all, the answer is called a 'real answer': if it is altered as described above, it is called a 'tonal answer'.

Since J. S. Bach generally preferred tonal answers, modern teachers are inclined to regard a tonal answer as indispensable, except in particular cases defined by rule. But Prout points out that Handel shows a great partiality for real answers, and Handel's authority is surely as good as anyone else's.

The underlying principle is that whatever notes in the subject belong to the tonic are given to the dominant in the answer, and that whatever notes in the subject belong to the dominant are given in the answer to the tonic.

The first thing, therefore, is to decide exactly where the subject ends, and when the end has been found, to see whether it ends in the tonic or the dominant. If the subject quite clearly ends in the tonic, it should generally have a real answer, in spite of temporary intermediate modulations. If it ends in the dominant, the answer must be made to end in the tonic. The question then arises: at what point is the mutation to be made?

Gédalge goes into this difficult question so fully as to leave no possibility of error; other writers are content with general principles. As I cannot print musical examples here, I must be more summary, but I hope the following suggestions will be helpful.

Bear in mind that the orthodox rule originated in times when fugues were almost always vocal and slow, generally to sacred words. If the dominant occurs as a single long note, it is answered by the tonic, because it is thought of as a bass note, bearing harmony on the top. If the dominant is a quick note, comparatively unimportant, it is more likely to call for a real answer. Examiners often seem quite unaware that the 'correct' answer to a fugue subject may depend on its *tempo*. If we remember the historical reason, it will help us to accustom our ear to the tonal answers of many classical fugues of the conventional type.

Gédalge suggests that the mutation will very often occur at the point where the 'head' can be separated from the 'tail'. This is a useful hint, but it will not always work.

The problem of the tonal answer has two aspects. (1) The case where a subject begins with emphatic tonic and dominant notes, e.g. doh soh lah soh in minims. Here the orthodox answer will be soh doh¹ me¹ ray¹. Note that it is not soh doh¹ me¹ doh¹; in these cases it has always been considered sufficient to answer the *first* important soh with a doh, continuing with a real answer. (2) The case where a subject definitely modulates to the dominant and ends in it. Here we must work backwards from the end to find the point at which the modulation occurs. In doing so we shall be guided partly by musical instinct, and always by the principle (laid down by Riemann and Prout) that all music (or

22

nearly all, in actual fact) is to be analysed into 'motives' consisting of an up-beat followed by a down-beat. In other words most music proceeds on the rhythmic system $4|\overset{\frown}{1}$, $\overset{\frown}{2}$ 3, $4|\overset{\frown}{1}$ and not on the system $|\overset{\frown}{1}$ 2, $\overset{\frown}{3}$ $4|$. It is the up-beat which does the work, and in harmony a dominant cadence has the dominant chord (e.g. dominant seventh) on the up-beat, and the final tonic on the down-beat: $\overset{2}{A}$-$|$-$\overset{1}{men}$, not $|\overset{1}{A}$-$\overset{2}{men}$ $|$.

Hence in considering a fugal answer we shall generally find that the point at which the mutation begins will be a weak beat rather than a strong one.

It is quite possible for cases (1) and (2) to occur in one and the same subject. Note that in the answer doh often has to represent both soh and fah in the subject. Consequently, if the subject has

$$|\text{ soh: soh, fah } |\text{ me, ray: doh }|$$

the tonal answer will be

$$|\text{ doh}^{\text{I}}\text{: doh}^{\text{I}}\text{, doh}^{\text{I}} |\text{ te, lah: soh }|$$

and *not*

$$|\text{ doh}^{\text{I}}\text{: ray}^{\text{I}}\text{, doh}^{\text{I}} |\text{ te, lah: soh }|$$

as we might well be tempted to write, thinking it more musical. It probably is; but it infringes the strict rule that the answer must never move in a direction contrary to that shown in the subject. If the subject moves downwards, the answer must either do the same or stand still on the same note; it must not under any circumstances move upwards. This rule may seem unmusical, but it is probably to be explained by the possibility of confusion with a deliberate *inversion* of the subject.

Answer by inversion is comparatively rare, but not on that account either incorrect or undesirable; the classical example is 'Egypt was glad' in Handel's *Israel in Egypt*. The beginner, however, will do well to leave answer by inversion until he is quite sure of himself as regards normal tonal answer.

Chromatic subjects as a rule have real answers, because the holding up of a note and repeating it would at once destroy the essential chromatic movement.

It is vitally necessary that the answer should make a good musical phrase, and if the result of obeying rules strictly is an ugly phrase which merely distorts and disfigures the expression of the subject, then it is certainly a wrong answer, and it is better to accept the situation, as Handel often does, and write a real answer.

A real answer may be right in what has been called above 'case (1)'; but in 'case (2)' a real answer is dangerous, because it leads to the supertonic instead of the tonic. But even this can be evaded by discreet modification, and by the insertion of a *codetta* which may perhaps bring in a new interest and expression.

CODETTAS

Codetta is diminutive of *coda* and means a little tail-piece. In fugue it means a little extra bit added on to subject or answer in order to fill up time, or in order to modulate to another key and make a better join with the next entry.

A *codetta* should grow naturally out of what precedes, but it is not to be regarded as a fixed theme, like a subject or counter-subject; it can be varied, lengthened, shortened or discarded as convenient. But it is all the better if it has *some* thematic character, and if it is to grow into an *episode*, thematic character becomes indispensable.

Codettas are easy enough to write in instrumental fugues, but often difficult in vocal fugues with words, because they may produce ludicrous repetitions or extensions which ruin the natural declamation of the words. This does not matter so much when the words are comparatively meaningless or conventional, e.g.

Hallelujah, amen, Kyrie eleison, &c., but as soon as the words have definite sense that demands *expression*, sacred or secular, whatever the language may be, the *codetta* becomes troublesome.

It is better to avoid *codettas* in these cases if possible. Rests are one solution of the problem; and in vocal fugues rests are more satisfactory and indeed more necessary than in instrumental, (1) because the words must determine the natural shape of a phrase, and so a well-set vocal phrase followed with a rest is more satisfactory than a vocal phrase awkwardly extended, (2) because singers require rests to take breath and to take real rest as well.

Handel and others of the 18th century, writing fugues with many semiquavers on a single syllable, can do what they like with *codettas*; but when Handel sets dramatic English words, as in his oratorios, he has to do without *codettas* as far as possible. In the chorus 'And with His stripes' (*Messiah*) the continuity is very skilfully preserved owing to the fact that the word 'healèd' can be treated either shortly, as in the first entry, or extended for several bars if necessary without offending good sense.

COUNTER-SUBJECT

The natural temptation is, not to think about the counter-subject until the moment when one requires it, i.e. on the first entrance of the answer, and then to leave its composition rather to instinct. The result is generally unsatisfactory. Gédalge advises us always to compose the counter-subject *on the subject* itself, because (he says) if we have to alter it to suit the tonal alteration of the answer, it is easier to do that than to alter it backwards to suit the shape of the subject.

We cannot take too much trouble over our counter-subject, whether vocal or instrumental. The first entry of it, along with the first entry of the answer, is the most exposed part of the whole fugue; it is the moment at which criticism is easiest and likely to be the most severe. In later entries both subject, answer and counter-subject may be more or less covered by the other parts; in any case it has always been allowed that they may be modified as the fugue proceeds. How far the 'great masters' allowed themselves such modification may be seen very startlingly in Prout's *Fugal Analysis*.

The double counterpoint of the counter-subject must be un-impeachable. If you find it difficult to write good double counter-point, begin by composing a counter-subject in *strict* counterpoint with no licenses, employing contrary motion as much as possible. You will quite likely find that you have written double counter-point without being aware of it. After you have written this, you can improve it by variations and the addition of notes in short values. It is hardly possible to lay down any general rules about the style of a counter-subject; but it is safe to say that it must make its own contribution to the *expressive* aspect of the fugue and not be content with mere double counterpoint.

In a vocal fugue the counter-subject will generally have different words, e.g.

> *Subj*. Og the King of Bashan:
>
> *C.S.* For his mercy endureth for ever.

The Psalms are a very useful source from which to take words for fugues, as the second half of any verse will naturally form the counter-subject.

It is very difficult at first to compose a counter-subject that fulfils both the indispensable conditions, (1) double counterpoint, and (2) proper expression and declamation of words. But this difficulty must be resolutely faced and conquered, for without doing this no satisfactory progress can be made with Fugue.

Gédalge further suggests that the counter-subject should not enter until after the 'head' of the subject, (1) because it thus leaves the (very important) 'head' more free to stand out, and (2) because if the *mutation* takes place after the 'head' the counter-subject will be easier to manage. He suggests that if necessary the 'head' should be accompanied by a variable *codetta* hanging over from the end of the first entry of the subject and repeated (as required) in subsequent entries.

Prout, in *Fugal Analysis*, devotes a section to fugues *without* a regular counter-subject. The beginner may think these are easier to write, but this is not the case. They require a great deal more invention, if they are to be any good, because the variable counter-subject must always be expressive, even if it is not regular, and being variable it will have to cover a much wider range of expression.

It is much better to begin one's studies with a regular counter-subject. It is also much safer in examinations, as examiners are not usually prepared to adapt their minds to fugues of the less common types.

But at the same time it is advisable to compose *more than one* counter-subject to the given subject. (1) This is good practice in itself, merely as an academic exercise; (2) it stimulates invention and suggests new possibilities of expression: (3) the invariable use of the same counter-subject all through a fugue of even moderate length becomes monotonous, and for middle entries an entirely new counter-subject may be a great help. It is all the better if it will work in double counterpoint. If it can be combined later on with the first counter-subject and made to work in triple counterpoint with it, better still—but this is perhaps more than one can ask from a beginner.

When a subject is rather conventional in style it may be possible to give it various interpretations, e.g. (1) resolute and energetic, (2) playful and coquettish, or (3) organist's jog-trot. The student should practise composing first a bare skeleton

27

counter-subject in the strict style, and then writing variations on it which will bring out different characteristics.

With regard to both subject and answer it is most important to envisage both as possible basses. Composers of Handel's time seem to have regarded every melody as a possible bass, witness the fact that in their solo cantatas the entrance of the voice, singing the most charmingly melodious theme, exquisitely suited to the expression of the words, will almost invariably be preceded by an introduction for the harpsichord in which the same melody is put into the bass and figured. It would be a pity to spoil a really expressive fugue-subject in order to make it more easily workable as a bass; but in composing a counter-subject one of the obvious difficulties is to make it satisfactory as a sound bass and at the same time melodious enough to take its place in the treble.

DOUBLE COUNTERPOINT IN THE TENTH AND TWELFTH

It is useful to know exactly what these things are and to be able to write them if required. But in practice, double counterpoint in the tenth reduces itself mainly to the device of doubling a subject or counter-subject in thirds or sixths. If you find that this is a procedure which suits your subject or counter-subject and heightens its effect, use it as you feel inclined, but there is really no great ingenuity about it. It is hardly worth while starting to write a counter-subject in double counterpoint in the tenth before you have begun to compose your fugue.

The same applies to double counterpoint in the twelfth, a device which is talked of by teachers as if it was a very occult mystery requiring profound study. Practise it if you like, for that will always help you to use it if you want it. The percentage of classical fugues in which it occurs must be small. In most cases it looks as if it had occurred by accident: the composer did not design it from the beginning, but found at a certain point that his old counter-subject happened to fit in the twelfth as well. The classical example of fugue with intentional and systematic double counterpoint in the twelfth is 'Let all the angels of God' in *Messiah*, when the counter-subject is also a diminution of the subject. The chief advantage gained by the device seems to be that the counter-subject is available for either subject or answer in the same convenient part of the voice's compass. If our double counterpoint is all in contrary motion and also conjunct, it will fit in almost any interval you like to experiment with, especially if you are not scrupulous about the rules of strict counterpoint.

Double counterpoint in the twelfth is most likely to be useful if we are writing an elaborate fugue with several subjects and counter-subjects and wish to combine as many of them as possible simultaneously to make a climax. In such moments subjects have generally to be squeezed in wherever they can be coaxed or forced to fit, and sometimes at the oddest intervals. This is always interesting, but hardly work for beginners, though beginners may well amuse (and instruct) themselves with making *quodlibets*. *Quodlibets* are very useful for comic opera and revue, &c., as they can be applied in a political sense.

EXPOSITION

The first difficulty of an exposition is the joining up of the various entries. Hence the importance of knowing definitely where a subject ends (as in vocal fugue it inevitably must, owing to the words). It is a mistake to suppose that a subject automatically— or (shall we say?) legally—reaches its end as soon as the next voice enters (see '48', Book I, fugue in F). An old rule which modern text-books seem to have forgotten is that when the subject ends in the tonic it must carefully avoid making an obvious move to the dominant in order that the answer may enter. The change of key must be disguised in some way. The same applies to all the entries; anything like a dead stop at the end of each entry must be avoided, and full closes are strictly forbidden by the old teachers. The joints must be covered up by deceptive cadences, suspensions and other devices. A mistake often made by beginners is to make a cadence on a common chord with the root at both top and bottom. If the root cannot be avoided in the lowest voice, care must be taken to make the top voice move at any rate to the third of the root, so as to secure continuity.

The older teachers of strict counterpoint forbade, in two-part counterpoint, or between the extreme parts in all counterpoints, the approach to the octave by contrary and conjunct motion, as

$$\left| \begin{array}{c|c} \text{ray}^\text{l} & \text{doh}^\text{l} \\ \text{te}_\text{l} & \text{doh} \end{array} \right|$$

in the course of a piece of music. This is called the *ottava battuta*. Rockstro mentions the rule, but appears not to have understood it, and many other teachers have been equally puzzled by it, or have thought it safer not to mention it. The reason for the rule is obvious: the forbidden progression is the normal final ending in all two-part counterpoint—the only ending allowed, in fact, either at the octave or at the unison. Hence, if it occurs anywhere else, it at once suggests to the hearer the effect of a full stop and an end where no end is intended. The rule therefore is still applicable to all composition, however modern, though it is not so strictly enforced, and a full close may be legitimate to mark the end of a section or chapter in a fugue.

If an exposition is built on a downward series of entries, the top voice presents difficulty to the beginner as soon as it has finished with the counter-subject against the answer in the next voice, i.e. at the third entry of the subject. It is urgently important that this treble voice should continue with a free part that is as melodious and interesting as possible. This is where the composer's real invention is needed. The ear inevitably listens to the topmost voice as the 'tune' of a piece of music, whether it be a fugue or anything else—even when the obvious 'tune' is in the bass and the treble is only playing an accompaniment. In a fugue it is most important that the free top part should never cease to be interesting, and indeed that it should always take the melodic lead. If it does not, the fugue will inevitably be dull; and that is the chief reason why so many fugues (including some by 'great masters') *are* dull.

If the exposition is built up from the bass, the situation as regards the bass part will be exactly the same, though less obviously so. Care must be taken that the bass part does not degenerate into a 'table-leg' bass, i.e. one which has no melodic interest and merely supports the harmony. The remedy for this is never to forget that the bass part must be *expressive*, and it cannot be expressive unless it is melodious. If the fugue has words, the sense of the words ought to force the composer into expressiveness; and the words will also tell him when to bring the part to a temporary end and give the singer a rest. But in instrumental fugues the beginner (as well as many who are by no means beginners) is invariably tempted to let the bass go on and on, becoming less and less interesting. This temptation must be carefully watched and vigorously resisted.

COUNTER-EXPOSITION

In some long fugues, and in some short two-part fugues of the vocal type as well, there is a counter-exposition. This may (in a four-part fugue) extend to all four voices, but is sometimes reduced to two entries, or even one. The only justification for a counter-exposition is that it should be more interesting than the initial exposition, and present the material of the fugue in a new light, contributing in some way to the general *expression* of the fugue.

A counter-exposition should not start with a single unaccompanied entry, like the exposition; the first voice which comes in should have one or more with it, to give it a new interest.

Some teachers have suggested that the object of a counter-exposition, or at any rate of a single additional entry, is to exhibit double counterpoint, to show the inversion of subject and counter-subject. So it is, but in more than a merely academic sense. If double counterpoint has any value at all, it must be an expressive value, and in that case the inversion really does make a new and important contribution to the expression of the fugue. This reason should never be lost sight of. A counter-subject which from the start has been heard only in an inferior voice (as when the exposition starts from the bass and works upwards) may (and ought to) take on a startlingly new expression when suddenly heard in the treble, above full harmony with the subject in the bass, and the more striking this new expression is, the more urgent it is that the feeling should not be let down by the treble then relapsing into something quite uninteresting. The mood must be kept up and perhaps intensified.

EPISODES

Episodes present considerable difficulty to a beginner, all the more if he has been told that episodes are the test of a composer's real inventive powers.

It is quite possible and reasonable to write a fugue without any episodes at all. The first fugue of the '48' is the classical example of this. Many of the vocal fugues in Mozart's church music have no episodes, or hardly any.

In many fugues of J. S. Bach, notably in the long organ fugues, the episodes are very important, and extremely free and imaginative, so that the episodes seem at times to be the most striking parts of the fugue. This shows the difference (pointed out in the introduction) between the 'Catholic' vocal fugue and the 'Protestant' organ fugue, which in the hands of Buxtehude, J. S. Bach and others has almost the freedom of an improvisation. It is obvious too that performers (e.g. Mendelssohn, Saint-Saëns, Bruckner) who publicly improvised fugues on the organ must have relied very largely on episodes.

The beginner will do well to start first on fugues without episodes. He will at once find that a *codetta* is a necessity now and then, however short, and it may interest him to lengthen his *codetta* as the fugue proceeds. If a *codetta* has to effect a modulation, it may well need extension, and out of such *codettas* episodes have come into being.

Even when writing episodes of some length and importance, it must never be forgotten that the first function of an episode is to *effect a modulation*. It is therefore most necessary that we should make up our minds first what key we wish to reach, and then to consider how to get there, and whether quickly or more indirectly and slowly. If the beginner does not take this decision and stick to it, he will easily find that the episode has led him unwittingly into some quite different key, with the result that the tonal scheme of the whole fugue is upset.

In vocal fugues the problem of finding words for episodes is often very difficult. Words in one's own language, and even words such as those of the Psalms in Latin, cannot be treated after the way in which the great masters have treated *Kyrie eleison*, &c.

If the words of the subject and counter-subject are repeated to different music, or chopped up, the result may easily be ridiculous. It is useful to have some more words in reserve, if possible. Here it may be pointed out that Mozart, in setting a long Psalm to music (e.g. in the Vespers), often gets over the ground quickly by using new words for each successive set of entries, using the same music of the original subject with the minimum of modification. As he is often able to introduce a great variety of *strettos*, inversions, &c., the fugue perpetually gains in interest and excitement. This however requires a high degree of skill and cannot be attempted as a first start.

Episodes offer good opportunity of reducing the number of voices taking part. If the fugue is in four parts, the episodes may well be mainly in three or sometimes even in two. If the fugue is in two parts only, an episode in one part is hardly possible, but in two-part fugues, especially in instrumental ones with rapid notes, it is most desirable to let each part have a rest of some length now and then while the other carries on alone, either with a new subject or with a continuation of the original one. I do not mean a mere repetition of the original subject, but a prolongation of it, growing naturally out of it.

Another thing to remember about episodes is that they can often help to break the rhythmical monotony of a fugue. If the subject is in a rhythm of four bars, the episodes may well be more 'choppy', in smaller rhythm, such as two bars or one. Again, if the subject happens to be a 'choppy' one itself, the episodes may well be made more continuous and flowing, with longer rhythmic periods. These suggestions apply mainly to instrumental fugues, but they are applicable to vocal fugues too on a smaller scale.

Triple counterpoint is very useful in episodes, because it enables the same material to be worked in many different ways: it will also help to disguise the obviousness of a sequence, when a series of sequences is used to effect a modulation. Sequences are rather out of fashion nowadays, but in the classical days they were the orthodox method of building episodes and effecting modulations, and the beginner will do quite well to practise them and learn to make them do what he wants.

MIDDLE ENTRIES

The nature and number of these will depend on the general plan of the fugue, and also on whether it is vocal or instrumental. On another page the general problem of form in Fugue is discussed (see also the section 'History of Fugue') and a few plans of various dimensions are suggested. Roughly speaking, the middle section of a fugue corresponds to the development section of a sonata-movement, and its length and importance, as well as its emotional significance, will depend on whether we are looking at sonata-form from Mozart's point of view or from Beethoven's. The middle entries, too, will have to be planned in relation to the episodes, if the fugue is a long one; another question that may arise is whether in this section the entries or the episodes are to be the more important. All these problems are more for the accomplished composer than for the beginner; but it is desirable that the beginner should know about them from the first and realize that even the smallest and most elementary forms of fugue are none the less essentially problems in expression.

In any case the middle section will probably aim at being more emotional, more exciting, more fantastic (to give the reader a small choice of epithets) than the exposition; it is like the second act of a play in three acts, where all the difficulties and complications arise. How can we attain this object in a fugue?

(1) We may present the subject in new keys. The orthodox rule is that we must not go too far afield, limiting ourselves to keys which would require not more than one new flat or sharp for the signature.

Thus, the only admissible keys will be those on the notes of the unaltered scale, omitting those which bear imperfect triads: in C major–C, D minor, E minor, F major, G major, A minor (not B minor); in C minor–C minor (not D minor), E flat major, F minor,

G minor, A flat major, B flat major. From a modern point of view this is a limited range, but it at any rate provides a well-balanced contrast of major and minor in each case. To go farther afield is hardly the 'beginner's' affair: but it may be noted here that cases may easily arise in which the change from major to minor or from minor to major will be inappropriate. If the fugue is very cheerful or very melancholy, the subject will not adapt itself to the change of mode, especially if there are very cheerful or very melancholy words. In such cases we may utilize the other mode by putting new or more suitable words to it, or we may decide to keep the original words and choose other keys in the same mode.

(2) We may introduce a new element by using a new counter-subject, which may or may not combine with the old one later on. Albrechtsberger says that when a fugue modulates to a new key the subject ought not to enter entirely alone, but should have at least one accompanying voice. This need not be a strict rule, but it is certainly useful advice.

(3) We may modify the subject, provided that the modification does not alter the subject too much, and provided that it clearly has expressive value and is intentional and purposeful, not a mere awkward accident.

(4) We may shorten the subject, or use part of it. This applies particularly to subjects of the Handelian type with a 'head' and 'tail'; sometimes the 'head' alone is used, and sometimes the 'tail' by itself, though the 'tail' generally lends itself more to treatment as material for episodes (cf. 'And he shall purify' in *Messiah*).

(5) We may cause the subject to enter by *stretto*; i.e. to let the second voice enter before the first voice has finished. Most text-books, ancient or modern, assume that *stretto* is always reserved for the final entries, but it may quite often happen that *stretto* is more suitable to the middle ones, and that the interest of the last section can be maintained better in some other ways. Not all

subjects will work in *stretto*, but the beginner should always take trouble to try out (on his rough sheet) all the possibilities that he can find.

(6) Inversion and augmentation or diminution, also usually reserved for the end, can often be used suitably in the middle.

(7) A dominant pedal will often make a good preparation for the final entries, and a *stretto* on a dominant pedal is always effective.

The important thing is to decide where we wish our emotional climax to come. Some fugues (especially organ fugues) make a *crescendo* to the end; others regard the final section as a gradual settling down to peace after a strenuous development section, and various schemes can be designed in between these two extremes. Here, as in every other part of a fugue, the formal construction is not a question of conventional rule, but fundamentally a problem of emotional expression. All musical form in fact, however much conventionalized by the habits of generations, is simply the problem of putting the most expressive moment in the most effective place.

FINAL ENTRIES

The fundamental necessity of the final section is that it should be more interesting than the exposition, and that it should sum up the whole expression of the fugue. Such devices as *stretto*, augmentation, inversion, &c., are not ends in themselves; they are merely means by which the desired effect may be secured. What suits one subject may be quite inappropriate to another.

Stretto is essentially a device for voices, and the closer the *stretto* is made, the less effective it becomes with instruments. A very close *stretto* is only effective (1) as the climax of a series of *strettos*, each closer than the last; (2) when the words start with an energetic and significant first syllable, as in Mozart's *Pignus futurae gloriae.* On the pianoforte or organ such a *stretto* makes no effect at all, though we try to pretend that it does in the B flat minor fugue of the '48', Book I, which is unusually vocal in character for J. S. Bach.

The chief drawback of *stretto* (noticeable especially in instrumental fugues) is that it 'telescopes' the rhythm. If a subject is two bars long and enters four times, the exposition will be eight bars long; if it enters in *stretto*, the total length of the entries may be reduced to four, two or even to a single bar, thus completely upsetting the general rhythm. This further tempts the beginner to make his final section much shorter than the exposition, so that owing to various difficulties the whole section falls lamentably flat instead of enhancing the general effect. This can sometimes be avoided by making two or more *strettos*, not necessarily closer and closer, but with different arrangement of voices, or reversing the order of keys (i.e. of subject and answer), so that one *stretto* leads from tonic to dominant and another from dominant to tonic.

When a *stretto* brings in each voice in strict canon for some appreciable time it is called a *stretto maestrale* (masterly). These are difficult and comparatively rare; they are mostly to be found in old church music of a very conventional type. The fact is that a *stretto maestrale* is hardly possible except with some very conventional and hackneyed subject.

All teachers of fugue, of whatever period or country, are agreed that in an ordinary *stretto* there is no need to continue exact imitation after the next voice has entered. Supposing we build up a *stretto* in the order bass, tenor, alto, treble: the moment Tenor enters, Bass may discard his subject and go where he pleases. Similarly, the moment Alto enters, Tenor may discard the subject, and Alto may do the same on the entry of Treble. But at this point the *stretto* becomes subject to a very stringent rule, viz. that the last entering voice (here Treble) must go on with the original subject to the end.

Beginners often find this difficult to understand and manage. They very generally and naturally imagine that the most important voice in a *stretto* is the one which enters first. It is only natural, in experimenting with a subject, that we should begin by writing it down complete in one voice (say the Bass) and then try how far we can induce Tenor to combine with it in canon at a short distance. Probably at some point we have to make a 'slight modification'. Then we try the Alto, with more inevitable modification, and finally the Treble, whose entry may be hardly recognizable as the subject at all. We may land ourselves in further trouble, for if the subject will not work in the octave, fourth or fifth, we may (and this is certainly not forbidden) try other keys with a little more success; but at the risk of arriving at some key which is not appropriate to the general harmonic situation.

The thing to remember is that in all *strettos* the most important voice is the *last* one, and that the previous entries are merely preliminaries to lead up to it, just as in a play subordinate characters come on to the stage first to prepare the entry of the hero or heroine, or in a ceremonial procession the king or archbishop does not walk first, but after various less important personages. (Compare Byrd's *Songs of Sadnesse and Pietie*, Palestrina's Hymns and J. S. Bach's Chorale Preludes.)

The rule is in fact based on human nature; when the second voice enters, anyone can recognize the imitation of the first, but the general public is incapable of following the further course of the previous voice, still more so after attention has been distracted by successive new entries of the subject.

As in the exposition, care should be taken that the last voice of a *stretto* should be either the Treble or the Bass (there are classical exceptions to this rule), as it is in outside positions that the complete subject will be best heard and recognized.

Augmentation often attracts beginners, as it is generally easy to manage. But augmentation is seldom effective except for voices, or for keyboard instruments. It is always effective on the pedals of the organ, but not much use to a violoncello or double bass. The organ can bring out an augmentation in the treble or even in a middle part by ingenious registration; with voices or other instruments an interior augmentation is seldom audible. Indeed, the final and most important entry of a subject is hardly ever effective in an inner part unless it makes a very strong rhythmical contrast with the others, e.g. a subject in minims against other parts in semiquavers, or vice versa.

Diminution will always work if augmentation will; but it is not often practicable or suitable in vocal fugues. It is mainly appropriate to the organ, which will stand a wider contrast of time-values than any other musical medium.

Inversion is sometimes interesting, but has no value in itself. It is effective only when the inversion is clearly recognizable to an audience and when it has some expressive significance. A merely mechanical inversion is as useless as a merely mechanical *cancrizans* (with all respect to Beethoven). Still, it is not at all impossible to recognize a gramophone record when it is played backwards, and *cancrizans* may yet have a new future.

Albrechtsberger, after explaining all forms of inversion, says that these things are useful because by such means a single idea (i.e. the subject) can be brought into the most varied positions and can lead to useful modulations. He advises the pupil to write out all the possible inversions of a theme and then to harmonize each separately as a bass with chords above. This of course is merely an instructive study, not part of a fugue in itself; and it is interesting as showing how the old composers, even as late as the beginning of the 19th century, had the ingrained habit of regarding every sort of melody as a potential bass.

Some subjects will not work in *stretto* at all happily, though if the method explained above be adopted ruthlessly it is obvious that there is no subject which will not work in *stretto*. Augmentation and inversion may be equally impracticable. What can we do to make our subject more interesting in the final section?

Variation and *extension* are both methods often exemplified in classical fugues. I use the word *extension* here as the equivalent of the German expression *fortspinnen*, which means the spinning of a long continuous thread like a spider. This is most easily done when the subject has already a long 'tail' of semiquavers; but it always runs the risk of degenerating into mere nonsense. In fact, the more interesting the subject is, the more difficult it is to 'spin it out', and while the German word *fortspinnen* conveys no disparaging sense, the English 'spinning-out' is always understood as something undesirable. But real extension or continuation is real invention, and should be studiously practised, for invention of this kind seldom comes without considerable effort of the imagination.

The choice of method to bring a fugue to an end depends to a certain extent on the nature of the subject and its adaptability to various devices, but far more on the expressive character of the whole fugue. The mere accumulation of ingenuities may be meritorious in the eyes of some examiners, but from an artistic point of view devices of this kind have no value unless they contribute to the emotional expression.

FUGUE AS A WHOLE

Stanford used to ask pupils, when they showed a decided natural facility for composition, to write fugues out of their own heads without worrying about orthodox rules. This task encourages personal expression, and is a good test of a pupil's abilities. It also shows the pupil where the difficulties of fugue begin; and the teacher, analysing the unsatisfactory passages of the pupil's fugue, can show him how a knowledge of the so-called rules would have helped him over the difficulties.

Academic rules may be divided into three classes: (1) those which are eternal psychological principles, applicable to all music; (2) those which are no more than the good manners of a particular period and may be quite wrong for another historical period; (3) those which are merely convenient 'dodges' for evading certain common difficulties. A teacher who makes rules into a cause of difficulty, and counterpoint into an 'obstacle-race', as Donald Tovey used to call it, does not know his business: the only use of rules is to explain and smooth away difficulties.

In the early stages of fugue-writing it is very desirable to adopt the good manners of an older century and to write for voices as far as possible in orthodox strict counterpoint. This suggestion is not to be taken too rigorously but only as a general principle.

One of the greatest difficulties to the beginner is the problem of form, i.e. of key-distribution, and I therefore set out here a few graded schemes, taken from various authorities, which will be useful for those who are still in the stage of sticking to a safe track and taking their difficulties step by step.

1

Elementary fugue in two parts (from Albrechtsberger) suitable for the strict vocal style, but also applicable to instruments. Subject in tonic, answer in dominant; no regular counter-subject. Both voices continue together for a few more bars, leading to a cadence on the dominant. Here the second voice leaves off, while the first voice continues with a *codetta*. Before the end of this the second voice, after a rest, enters with the original subject in the tonic; the first voice follows with the answer at a shorter interval. Again both continue for a few bars more to a cadence in the (minor) key of the mediant. The first voice then enters again with the subject in the tonic, answered in close *stretto* by the second voice, after which a considerably longer extension brings the fugue to an end.

This type of fugue does not involve any double counterpoint, but requires two features which the beginner often finds difficult, *stretto* and the free continuation of a theme; both these things should be mastered as early as possible.

2

Classical church music shows many examples of short choral fugue-movements occurring in the course of a Mass or other long work. These generally consist of an exposition (four voices) followed either by one more entry of the subject in the tonic, or by a short and sometimes incomplete *stretto*, after which there is a *coda*. In such movements it has obviously been the composer's aim to compress a fugue into the shortest possible limits (cf. the two different *Osanna* fugues in Mozart's *Requiem*).

3

When the saving of time in performance is not an urgent consideration, and especially when the fugue is in less than four parts, a satisfactory design may be obtained by including a short middle section. This may be preceded and followed by episodes, or not, as may be more suitable to the general style. The short middle section may have two entries in new keys, or even one. If the exposition leads strongly towards the dominant, this middle entry should emphasize the subdominant; if the exposition keeps more to the tonic, it would be better to use a subsidiary minor key for the middle entry, assuming the fugue to be in a major key. If the fugue is in a minor key, the choice between subdominant (minor) and relative major (or other major key) will be determined chiefly by the expressive character of the fugue.

The most useful type of fugue for academic practice is that suggested by Gédalge, based on the rules of Cherubini and accepted as the standard form by the Paris Conservatoire. Outside that institution there is no need for students to regard it as strictly obligatory, even in examinations; but for those who are not yet sure of themselves as regards form it is a safe guide and presents the minimum of difficulty.

FUGUE IN A MAJOR KEY

Exposition in tonic and dominant. Episode leading to middle section: entries of subject and answer in the relative minor and its (minor) dominant. After another episode, entry in subdominant. This must not be answered at the fifth, as that would bring us back to the tonic too soon; the answer is therefore made in the key a third below, i.e. the supertonic (minor). At Paris it is here customary to make an episode leading to a pause on the chord of the dominant; but elsewhere this need not be obligatory, as long as a return is made to the tonic as a centre for the final entries, ending with a *coda*.

FUGUE IN A MINOR KEY

Exposition in tonic and dominant. Episode leading to middle entries in relative major and its dominant; after another episode, entries in subdominant (here major) and the key a third above, i.e. submediant (major); return through dominant to the tonic for final entries and *coda*.

Note that in each of these schemes the subdominant comes in the same place, and that the balance of major and minor keys is carefully preserved.

These two schemes, which form satisfactory complete fugues, may be easily remembered by memorizing the following melodies, as if they were chimes of bells. (They are written out

with bars merely because a rhythmical shape will make them
easier to learn and remember.)

Major: | : d¹ | s : l | m : f | r : s | d : — | — : — |
Minor: | : l₁ | m : d | s : r | f : m | l₁ : — | — : — |

The final note in each case is supposed to represent the entire
final section.

Palestrina's counterpoint as now taught is of no use for Fugue;
the counterpoint required is that of Fux, Cherubini, &c., as
habitually practised by such composers as Handel, Haydn and
Mozart. Dissonances should always be properly prepared. Pupils
with some knowledge of J. S. Bach often try to reproduce his
harmonic colour, using attractive dissonances without preparation.
This comes of playing J. S. Bach on the pianoforte; it is only by
singing ourselves that we can learn the emotional value of prepared suspensions. A student who sings in a chorus will learn far
more about counterpoint and fugue (assuming that he sings
Handel, J. S. Bach, &c.) than he will by playing these things on
the pianoforte or organ.

It is noticeable that even comparatively modern composers,
such as Liszt and Saint-Saëns, tend to drop into the 'Bach style'
as soon as they write fugues. It is really the Frescobaldi style,
and it certainly dominated orthodox fugue for two centuries, so
that even now it is singularly difficult to break away from it. That
is the certain duty of the modern composer, but the beginner will
find the task quite beyond him and he may leave it out of consideration until he has said good-bye to examinations.

COMMON ERRORS

Certain mistakes are very commonly made by beginners, and
should be noted and guarded against.

(1) The error of the *ottava battuta* already mentioned, i.e. in
general practice, the arrival on a common chord, on a strong beat,

with the key note at both top and bottom. Wherever this occurs it should be altered, if possible, as it suggests an end in the wrong place.

(2) Thin harmony. This comes of thinking harmonically rather than contrapuntally. Harmony in three or two parts will sound satisfactory only when the individual parts have great vitality of movement. The mere effort to secure complete triads in three parts will force the parts into movement to some extent, but the more inward movement they have of their own, the more they will be able to make this harmony sound satisfactory. In four parts there is no excuse whatever for thin harmony.

(3) In three parts (and even in four) chords of the sixth are often dangerous. It seems fatally easy, in Fugue, to write 'chords' which contain a sixth and nothing else. The question then arises; does this 6 imply a 6/3 or a 6/4? If it is to imply a 6/4 the bass must follow the orthodox rule. But in the Frescobaldi style a bare 6 would more naturally imply a 6/3 and the student must accustom himself (by the study of Corelli, Handel, &c.) to accepting this 6/3 as a matter of course. It is part of the 'good manners of the period'. More often the bare 6 seems to imply nothing and leave the hearer in a state of complete indecision as to the tonality.

Uncomfortable sixths often arise owing to the inversion of double counterpoint. We must therefore guard against them carefully when composing a double counterpoint and consider what it is going to sound like when inverted.

(4) Crossing of parts. In fugues for voices the parts may cross freely, subject to certain restrictions. The subject and counter-subject should never cross each other, least of all when they are heard together for the first time. If vocal parts cross, they must still remain within their practicable compass, and regard must be paid to the quality of voices in different registers. It is often dangerous to let the bass cross above the tenor, because the bass

voice in a high register is apt to be loud and aggressive, while the tenor's low notes are far too weak to support the general harmony.

Wind instruments may cross freely in the same way, because their tone-qualities are different enough to make the separate voices clear. This is not always the case with stringed instruments, though the viola and violoncello will always stand out in certain registers. Two violin parts which cross will easily destroy each other's melodic line, unless they are very sharply differentiated in rhythm.

Crossing parts is legitimate on the organ or harpsichord when the music is so written that the two parts can be played on separate manuals with contrasting stops. Otherwise it should be carefully avoided, and in writing fugues for the pianoforte the crossing of parts should be regarded as absolutely forbidden. This does not apply to the crossing of hands; but this, in contrapuntal writing, generally aims at producing the illusion of an additional voice.

(5) Change of style. If we never lose sight of the expressive character of a fugue we shall not begin it in one style and end it in another, e.g. beginning as a light and cheerful fugue for string quartet and ending as if it was a solemn fugue for organ.

It is fatally easy in fugue-writing (as J. S. Bach often showed) to relapse into the organ style without being aware of it. Those who play the organ should take particular care to guard against this unless definitely composing for their own instrument.

www.ingramcontent.com/pod-product-compliance
Ingram Content Group UK Ltd.
Pitfield, Milton Keynes, MK11 3LW, UK
UKHW042149280225
455719UK00001B/213